Praying

The Lord's Prayer:

Hope for the Neighborhood

Dewey Johnson

1

The Greatest of These is Clarity

When I pray The Lord's Prayer I say, *"Hallowed be thy name."* What does that mean? What does it mean to hallow anything, much less a name? God could answer my prayer and I'd totally miss it because I don't know what I'm asking. And which name? Lord, God Almighty, Creator, Elohim, El Shaddai, Father?

And how would I like it if God ruled fully? *"Your kingdom come"*, I pray, but if it did could I still take walks, tell jokes, make love, drink wine, and go to the movies? Is the new world coming more fun than I'm having now? It might be better to postpone it until I'm on my deathbed, for if the truth be told, I have things pretty good presently.

And what kind of bread are we talking? A Porsche costs a lot of bread. If I pray, *"Give us this day our daily bread"*, is there enough dough for me to make payments? What if I gathered a group of friends to go in with me and prayed instead, "Give us this day a winning Powerball ticket!" If we could win a big enough lottery, we'd be set for life. God wouldn't have to provide for us day after day.

And here's one that perplexes. Why do some Christians, including Methodists, pray, *"Forgive us our trespasses"*, while others, including Presbyterians, say, *"Forgive us our debts"*?

Two small congregations, one Presbyterian the other Methodist, held joint services one summer due to low attendance that time of the year. These were held at the Methodist church building. As summer came to an end, a layperson said during morning announcements, "It has been a great summer meeting together, but next Sunday you Presbyterians have to go back to your debts, while we Methodists stay here with our trespasses."

Which had I rather do, persist in my trespasses or face up to my debts?

And what's this about *Lead us not into temptation*? On the one hand, God wants me to obey the commandments, but on the other, if I'm not on my guard, God would tempt me to disobey? What kind of a God is that? Comedian Flip Wilson's character "Geraldine" made more sense. She used to say about her bad behavior, "The devil made me do it!"

Clarity in prayer is essential. One time a televangelist was hiking in the mountains when he startled two bears. Angered by his intrusion, they began chasing him. He ran for his life, the bears in hot pursuit. He ran and he ran, the bears still giving chase. Finally, he was so tired and winded that he fell to the ground and voiced the prayer he had prayed so many times over the years, "Lord, make them Christians!"

Suddenly the bears stopped in their tracks, dropped down on their knees, put their paws together, gazed into the heavens and prayed, "Lord, bless this food to the nourishment of our bodies and us to Christ's service. Amen"

I need to know exactly what it is that I'm praying for because, like the televangelist, I just might get it.

When it comes to The Lord's Prayer, clarity in prayer is dependent upon clarity of understanding Matthew 6: 9b-13, the passage of scripture that gives us The Lord's Prayer. In the study that follows, I have tried to avoid the piñata approach to scripture. It is so tempting. Take a blind swing here and a blind swing there in the hopes of God raining down insight. It doesn't work very well, though.

Instead, I have sought to understand where the words Jesus spoke came from in the history of those who first heard them, and then what other scriptures help shed light on their meaning. In this manner, I hope to clarify what it is we're praying for.

2

The Lord's Prayer in English

There are a number of English versions of The Lord's Prayer, Matthew 6: 9b-13. Here is a sampling.

The King James Version of the Bible (KJV):
Our Father, which art in heaven, Hallowed be thy name. Thy kingdom come. Thy will be done in earth, as it is in heaven. Give us this day our daily bread. And forgive us our debts, as we forgive our debtors. And lead us not into temptation, but deliver us from evil: For thine is the kingdom, and the power, and the glory, forever. Amen

The New International Version (NIV):
Our Father in heaven, hallowed be your name, your kingdom come, your will be done, on earth as it is in heaven. Give us today our daily bread. Forgive us our debts, as we also have forgiven our debtors. And lead us not into temptation, but deliver us from the evil one.

The New Revised Standard Version (NRSV):
Our Father in heaven, hallowed be your name. Your kingdom come. Your will be done, on earth as it is in heaven. Give us this day our daily bread. And forgive us our debts, as we also have forgiven our debtors. And do not bring us to the time of trial, but rescue us from the evil one.

4

The Jerusalem Bible (JB):

Our Father in heaven, may your name be held holy, your kingdom come, your will be done, on earth as in heaven. Give us today our daily bread. And forgive us our debts, as we have forgiven those who are in debt to us. And do not put us to the test, but save us from the evil one.

The Our Father or Pater Noster (also used by many Protestants):

Our Father, who art in heaven, hallowed be thy name, thy kingdom come, thy will be done, on earth as it is in heaven. Give us this day our daily bread, and forgive us our trespasses, as we forgive those who trespass against us, and lead us not into temptation, but deliver us from evil.

The Lord's Prayer (used by fewer Protestants):

Our Father, who art in heaven, hallowed be thy name, thy kingdom come, thy will be done, on earth as it is in heaven. Give us this day our daily bread, and forgive us our debts, as we forgive our debtors. And lead us not into temptation, but deliver us from evil.

The Good News Bible (GNB):

Our Father in heaven: May your holy name be honored; may your Kingdom come; may your will be done on earth as it is in heaven. Give us today the food we need. Forgive us the wrongs we

have done, as we forgive the wrongs that others have done to us.
Do not bring us to hard testing, but keep us safe from the Evil One.

The Message (M):
Our Father in heaven, reveal who you are. Set the world right;
Do what's best – as above, so below. Keep us alive with three
square meals. Keep us forgiven with you and forgiving others.
Keep us safe from ourselves and the devil. You're in charge! You
can do anything you want! You're ablaze in beauty! Yes. Yes. Yes.

The English versions above are translations of the original Greek text. Below is a copy of that text (transliterated). It is found in The Greek New Testament, a publication of United Bible Societies:

Pater hemon ho en tois ouranois, hagiastheto to onoma sou, eltheto he basileia sou, genetheto to thelema sou, hos en ouranoi, kai epi ges;
Ton arton hemon ton epiousion dos hemin semeron; kai aphes hemin ta opheilemata hemon, hos kai hemeis aphakamen tois opheiletais hemon; kai me eisenegkeis hemas eis peirasmon, alla rhusai hemas apo tou ponerou.

Question:

1. The King James Version reads, *Lead us not into temptation.*
   Other translations can differ. *Do not put us to the test* (JB), and
   Keep us safe from ourselves and the devil (M). List other

differences found in the versions above. In your opinion, how many of these are significant?

· · · · · · ·

As mentioned in Chapter 1, one of the most noticed differences is *Forgive us our debts* as opposed to *Forgive us our trespasses.* Why this difference?

My understanding is that a mistake was made by William Tyndale in 1525 while translating the New Testament into English. The New Testament Greek word for *trespasses, paraptomata,* is not found in The Lord's Prayer. He translated *opheilemata,* which means debts and is in TLP, as *trespasses.*

One little mistake, but then Thomas Cranmer perpetuated it by using Tyndale's version of TLP in The Book of Common Prayer in 1549. It became the rage, so much so that by 1662 The Book of Common Prayer read:

Our Father, which art in heaven, hallowed be thy name; thy kingdom come; thy will be done, in earth as it is in heaven. Give us this day our daily bread. And forgive us our trespasses, as we forgive them that trespass against us. And lead us not into temptation; but deliver us from evil. For thine is the kingdom, the power, and the glory, Forever and ever. Amen

Over the centuries both *debts* and *trespasses* have become entrenched. For example, as a youngster in church on Sundays I read the King James Version of the Bible, which points out my *debts.* Then I went to public elementary school on weekdays where each day began with intercom announcements from the principal.

They were always preceded by the words, "But first, put your head down on your desk for the prayer."

The principal then played a 78 RPM record of TLP sung by a woman. I never knew the songstress' name, but five days a week for the first six years of public school I listened to her sing, *"Forgive us this day our trespasses as we forgive those who trespass against us."*

Not only was this my introduction to the concept of boundaries, but that of many other kids also. Teenagers on occasion forgot what they had heard her sing in elementary school and "trespassed and entered". Some were caught by the police and sent home to their parents. Even though their trespasses weren't that great, they had to attend Trespassers Anonymous meetings. Those whose trespasses were more substantial were sent to reform school and became known as juvenile delinquents. There they prayed, *"Forgive us our trespasses,"* until they had paid their debt to society. Is it any wonder the wording of this prayer is confusing? By trespassing they incurred a debt.

But trespassing is a kind of debt – I owe God better – and the word in TLP is *opheilemata,* which clearly means debts, *Forgive us our debts.*

Jesus does use the word *paraptoma,* trespasses, in a comment immediately following TLP:

"For if ye forgive men their trespasses (paraptomata), your heavenly Father will also forgive you: But if ye forgive not men their trespasses, neither will your Father forgive your trespasses." Matthew 6: 14, 15 (KJV)

I know people who refuse to say either trespasses or debts. They say, *"Forgive us our sins."* And they're right, in general.

8

Both trespasses and debts are kinds of sins. Here is yet another translation.

New Century Version
Our Father in heaven, may your name always be kept holy. May your kingdom come, and what you want be done, here on earth as it is in heaven. Give us the food we need for each day. Forgive us for our sins, just as we have forgiven those who sinned against us. And do not cause us to be tempted, but save us from the Evil One. Amen

The Customary Ending

For thine is the kingdom and the power and the glory forever, which most often concludes TLP in worship services, is found in the King James Version, but not in most English translations of the Bible. Nor is this conclusion found in the printed Greek New Testament text of Matthew 6: 9b-13. It is similar to David's farewell prayer in 1 Chronicles 29:10-19, especially vss.11 and 12. It seems to have been added later for embellishment, and is not a concern of this study.

Luke's Version of The Lord's Prayer

The Gospel of Luke contains a shorter account of The Lord's Prayer:

Father, hallowed be your name. Your kingdom come. Give us each day our daily bread. And forgive us our sins, for we ourselves forgive everyone indebted to us. And do not bring us to the time of trial. Lk.11: 2-4 (NRSV)

Question:

2. What major difference do you see between Luke and Matthew? TLP in Luke is not a concern of this study.

. . . .

3

The Immediate Context of The Lord's Prayer

The Lord's Prayer is the third most popular prayer in many parts of the world. The first two, in no particular order, are:

- "Thank You, thank You, thank You!"
- "Help me, help me, help me!"

Just as these two come in a context – that of gratitude and need – so The Lord's Prayer comes in a context.

Jesus said: *"And when you pray, do not imitate the hypocrites: they love to say their prayers standing up in the synagogues and at the street corners for people to see them. I tell you solemnly, they have had their reward. But when you pray, go into your private room, and when you have shut your door, pray to your Father who is in that secret place, and your Father who sees all that is done in secret will reward you.*

"In your prayers do not babble as the pagans do, for they think that by using many words they will make themselves heard. Do not be like them, for your Father knows what you need before you ask him. So you should pray like this:

"Our Father in heaven, hallowed be your name, your kingdom come, your will be done, on earth as it is in heaven. Give us today our daily bread. Forgive us our debts, as we also have forgiven our debtors. And lead us not into temptation, but deliver us from the evil one." Matthew 6: 5-13 (NIV)

A question brought up by the immediate context is this: if God already knows what I need – *your Father knows what you need before you ask him* – why pray? Because I may know what I want but not necessarily what I need.

In their song, *You Can't Always Get What You Want,* the Rolling Stones get it right. "You can't always get what you want. But if you try sometimes, yeah, you just might find you get what you need."

One thing that happens when I pray TLP is that God works to change me into a person who better distinguishes needs from wants. I may want all sorts of things, but what I need is the love required to be a good neighbor. I need the faith to trust that I have enough. I need the motivation to be actively involved in helping others. I need the grace to forgive. I need the courage to choose God's way rather than the ways of the world. I need the patience to wait for God's guidance. In short, I need to be put right with God.

Of my own merit, there is nothing right with my relationship to God. I am not, as Ferris Bueller's peers thought of him in the movie *Ferris Bueller's Day Off*, a "righteous dude". Time after time I think, speak, and behave in ways that obscure or betray my faith. Instead of the scribble I make of my basic beliefs, I need God's guidance and a clean slate daily.

There is always a struggle of agendas in prayer, mine versus God's, wants versus needs. When I set aside my agenda and choose God's way, then I'm being put right with God. Time and time again.

Note that The Lord's Prayer is a private prayer. Jesus says, *"But when you pray, go into your private room, and when you have shut your door, pray to your Father who is in that secret place."*

Many people voice TLP in worship services. That's why it's the third most popular prayer in some parts of the world. But why not also in private? I'm not against reciting TLP in worship – in my opinion it also has a place in a corporate context – but too often in worship services I hurry through the words without adequately thinking about what they mean.

In private I have the opportunity to spend more time with this prayer, think about what I'm saying. I can ponder the situations in my life addressed by the words. I can receive the guidance of an all-knowing, all-seeing God. Simone Weil, who after learning The Lord's Prayer in Greek, used it in her personal devotions. She said, "At times the very first words tear my thoughts from my body and transport them to a place outside space where there is neither perspective nor point of view." (1)

Jesus also warns us above about being hypocritical. *"And when you pray, do not imitate the hypocrites: they love to say their prayers standing up in the synagogues and at the street corners for people to see them."*

"Hypocrite" in Jesus' day was a word for an actor, say, a person who acts before others as though she is right with God of her own merit. (The Church Lady on Saturday Night Live?) A hypocrite would see no need to be put right with God.

I don't think that when I recite TLP in a worship setting I'm being hypocritical. But I do think that saying the prayer regularly in private heightens my awareness of what is being said. It also increases my awareness that what is being said is directed to God and involves me.

"When you pray, go into your private room, and when you have shut your door, pray to your Father who is in that secret

13

place, and your Father who sees all that is done in secret will reward you."

God not only knows a poor performance when God sees it, but as my life comes under God's gaze in prayer, God critiques my thoughts, words, and deeds. This gives me the opportunity to get the next act right rather than continue a disastrous performance such as a hypocrite (actor) might give. In this manner, I am being put right with God, which is the reward.

Questions:

3. The pagans in Matthew 6 (above) seem to think that their god(s) will eventually grant them a hearing if they what? How is the God of Jesus different?

4. Do you think that God answers some prayers but not others? Would knowing what God is on record as providing and not providing increase your confidence in prayer?

5. How does receiving what you need, as opposed to want, help you live in right relationship with God?

6. What is the reward of the hypocrites in vs. 5?

7. It is said that in prayer only the truth will do. Do you agree?

....

There are several ways to define sin. One is giving God less than God's due. I owe God better than I've given, and therein I have incurred a debt. The result is not being right with God. Sin also leads to my not being right with self, others, and the created world. The Bible highlights this alienation in Genesis 3-11.

God creates a productive, orderly world in Genesis 1 & 2 for the man and woman to enjoy and oversee. Instead, the man and woman, a.k.a. Adam and Eve, disobey the only prohibition on the books. They eat from the tree of the knowledge of good and evil, and after so doing come to realize that they owe God better than what they've given. Their sin estranges them from God. *"The man and his wife hid themselves from the presence of the Lord God among the trees of the garden."* Genesis 3: 8b (NRSV)

Not only do they hide from God, but there is a change of consciousness. Each becomes alienated from self, uncomfortable. *"Then the eyes of both were opened, and they knew that they were naked; and they sewed fig leaves together and made loincloths for themselves."* Genesis 3: 7. This leads to wearing Fig Leafs of the Loom and eventually to Gucci Outside the Garden. Some call this self-estrangement the Full-Employment Act for Psychiatrists.

Furthermore, humankind is estranged from nature. *"Cursed is the ground because of you; in toil you shall eat of it all the days of your life."* Genesis 3: 17c. Nature responds to the damage done by our sin with drought, flooding, scorching heat waves, boll weevils, locusts, hurricanes, weeds taking over our gardens, and even Bermuda grass sprouting up in the cracks in the concrete.

Adam and Eve's alienation from God then spreads to encompass the next generation, their sons. In Genesis 4, Cain the killer murders his brother Abel, who wasn't able to defend himself. Proof of our alienation one person from another. "Can't we just get along?" asked Rodney King. Apparently not. This has led to employment, even overtime in some instances, for police, lawyers, judges, security alarm salespeople, and marriage counselors.

In Genesis 11, the story of the Tower of Babel, humankind's sin results in peoples estranged from peoples, one category being nation versus nation. Peoples no longer speak the same language and there is no trust. This has resulted in Homeland Security, diplomats, red states and blue states, bugging devices, liberals versus conservatives, Main Street versus Wall Street, nuclear bombs, and a booming business for armament manufacturers.

When it comes to sin, I owe God better for the ways in which I'm estranged from God, alienated from self, on the outs with others, a polluter of the created world, and a participant in my people's hatred toward other peoples.

Questions:

8. In a movie based on real life, *Straight Story*, Alvin Straight and his brother quarreled and parted ten years earlier. They said "unforgivable things" and haven't communicated since. But then Alvin hears that his brother has had a stroke. Suddenly he is compelled to make-up with him. Because he doesn't have a driver's license and doesn't trust bus drivers, he rides a riding lawnmower across Iowa to his brother's house. Have you ever been moved in prayer or by an event to a reconciliation that you wouldn't have attempted earlier? Read Matthew 5: 23, 24

9. Alvin and his brother exemplify person estranged from person. What other examples stand out in your mind? Also of humans alienated from God? Of humans from nature? Of individuals from self? Of peoples not right with peoples?

....

16

4

Our Father in Heaven (the Addressee)

Our

Our is unexpected. Given that this is a private prayer, it makes sense to address this prayer to "My Father in heaven". Or to "My God", or to "My Lord". Why does Jesus have these other people, *Our*, cluttering up my private prayer?

A greater context of The Lord's Prayer than Matthew 6: 5-13 is the entire Christian Bible, which tells the story of the good that God has done, is doing, and will be working for all the peoples of the earth, not just some. Since God's love is for all, and not just me, the possessive case My doesn't do the job. *Our*, though, works to this end by reminding me that not only am I a member of Jesus' church, but I'm also a member of the human race. I pray as a member of both groups.

Our in the addressee section refers to all human beings, whether one follows Jesus or not, whether one believes in God or not. Us, which makes its appearance later in the prayer, refers to those who do follow Jesus. As a Christian, I am one of a people who, because we follow his teachings and example, are obligated to love all humankind, love defined as, *"Always treat others as you would like them to treat you."* Mt. 7:12 (JB)

Or stated another way, when Jesus was asked which of the commandments is the greatest, he said, *"'Love the Lord your God with all your heart and with all your soul and with all your mind.' This is the first and greatest commandment. And the second is like it: 'Love your neighbor as yourself.'"* Mt. 22: 37-39 (NIV)

And who is my neighbor? My tendency is to conveniently define neighbor as the person who looks, thinks, and acts like me. A person I'm already inclined to feel comfortable around. But this is not what Jesus meant. Neighbor, as he uses the word, is no less inclusive than the word *Our*. Everyone is Jesus' neighbor, everyone is loved by God, regardless of how she looks, thinks, and acts.

Jesus loves the little children, all the children of the world. Red, brown, yellow, black, and white, they are precious in his sight, Jesus loves the little children of the world. (When I first learned this song, we left out "brown". Can't do that.)

Our also links followers of Jesus to God's promise to Abraham (a.k.a. Abram):

Leave your country, your family, and your father's home for a land that I will show you. I'll make you a great nation and bless you. I'll make you famous; you'll be a blessing. I'll bless those who bless you; those who curse you I'll curse. All the families of the Earth will be blessed through you. Genesis 12: 1-3 (M)

Because I believe that Jesus is the fulfillment of this promise to Abraham, I'm to follow Jesus in the work of being a blessing as I love neighbor as self in no less a neighborhood than the entire world. There is no one who doesn't live on Jesus' block.

When I was in college I played a four-person card game called spades. Some dorm denizens personalized their score sheet, making columns like Dewey & Joe Don versus Curty & Jay Bob. My crowd didn't. We used the down-home headings Usins versus Urins, which was relative depending on who kept score. Years later, as I reflect upon the reality of how people treat and mistreat

18

each other, these headings sum it up accurately. Humankind mindlessly and arrogantly goes about life on planet earth as though we are aligned in groupings of Usins versus Urins. This as opposed to one humanity, *Ourins.*

Jesus taught a different way of living with others. He told a parable to some who were so proud of themselves that they figured it was alright with God for them to be contemptuous of others. The parable was about two men who went to the temple to pray.

One prayed like this, *"God, I thank you that I'm not like other people* (pick from the following Urins: Conservatives, Liberals, Muslims, Jews, Democrats, Republicans, Evangelistic Christians, Roman Catholics, Feminists, Good Ole Boys, Yuppies, Lesbians, Gays, Straights, Afro-Americans, Hispanics, Trailer trash, Wall Street Investment Banker Trash, Fill-in-the-blank _____ , *thieves, rogues, adulterers, or even like this tax collector.*

"I fast twice a week: I give a tenth of all my income."

The other fellow, standing apart, would not even look up toward heaven, but browbeat himself, saying, *"God be merciful to me a sinner!"*

Jesus said, *"I tell you, this man went down to his home justified* (or put right with God) *rather than the other; for all who exalt themselves will be humbled, but all who humble themselves will be exalted."* From Luke 18:9-14 (NRSV)

Questions:

10. What is difficult for you when it comes to regarding all humankind as your neighbors? Mr. Rogers didn't have clergypersons in his neighborhood. Who do you prefer to leave out of yours?

11. The task of Jesus' church is to represent the *Ourin* point of view. Is this your experience of the church?

12. Does *treating others as you would have them treat you* necessarily obligate you to agree with another's point of view or approve of another's choices or go along with what your neighbor might ask of you? How do you expect to be treated by your neighbors regardless of your differences?

....

Father

Jesus calls God *Father*, but not just any understanding of the name will do. The following teaching helps clarify the nature of Our *Father:*

"Look at the birds of the air; they do not sow or reap or store away in barns, and yet your heavenly Father feeds them. Are you not much more valuable than they?" Mt. 6: 26 (NIV)

It is Our *Father's* nature to value each and every human being and provide for Our needs, just as the best of parents value and provide for their children. No one else has as great a commitment to Our wellbeing. No one else adequately understands us and can provide Our needs.

Furthermore, Our *Father's* caring nature is not an iffy thing. God gives nothing but that which produces Our wellbeing. The Letter of James says about God's giving:

"Every generous act of giving, with every perfect gift is from above, coming down from the Father of lights, with whom there is no variation due to a shadow of turning." James 1: 17 (NRSV)

God, who is known in the Bible for a countenance that shines like the sun, never gives any of his children the cold shoulder, never turns his face away. And if there is *no variation due to a shadow of turning*, I can count on God's full attention, God at work for my wellbeing by providing a *perfect gift*, one that fits my need.

I can also count on God not playing favorites. Our *Father* has a whole world full of children, each of whom is loved as though he/she is an only child.

My brothers, as believers in our Lord Jesus Christ, the Lord of glory, you must never treat people in different ways according to their outward appearance. Suppose a rich man wearing a gold ring and fine clothes comes to your meeting, and a poor man in ragged clothes also comes. If you show more respect to the well-dressed man and say to him, "Have this best seat here," but say to the poor man, "Stand over there, or sit here on the floor by my feet," then you are guilty of creating distinctions among yourselves and of making judgments based on evil motives. James 2: 1-4 (GNB)

Question:

13. Do you believe that some of God's children are treated less well than others of God's children? By whom? Our *Father* or others? In what ways?

. . . .

If God's nature is that of a Father, it follows that ours is like that of children. Some find it offensive to think of themselves as a child. But there is a difference between being childish or immature, and being child-like, one who relies upon the parent for what is needed to live fully.

A child who wants his parents to buy him candy or ice cream as the family strolls though the mall, and who throws a tantrum to get it, is childish. A young child who gets lost in the mall, and who then is found by security personnel is child-like because he knows what he needs. "Where's my mommy!"

Some people are of the opinion that to think of oneself as a child of God implies a naivety stemming from an inferior brain or inferior education or both. But followers of Jesus strive to make the most of God's gift of the mind. In the New Testament, Paul had few intellectual equals, and Jesus said to his followers, *"I am sending you out like sheep into the midst of wolves. Therefore be as shrewd as snakes and as innocent as doves,"* Mt. 10:16.

It has long been said that the glory of God is a fully-alive human being. And what would a fully-alive human being look like? Something like a child of Our Father. In the world of the Bible, a child reflects the character of the father and carries on the interests of the father. As regards *Our Father*, this requires a maturity of mind, body, and spirit which Jesus invites me to gain by learning and practicing his ways. But I will never fully attain self-sufficiency. I will always be reliant upon the One who values me and provides for my needs, including putting me right when I'm not.

22

Questions:

14. Archie Manning became a well-respected pro football quarterback while playing for the New Orleans Saints. From the biblical point of view, what might it mean to be a son of Archie Manning? A son or daughter of Henry Fonda?

15. If you were off-the-charts smart – and please excuse me if you already are – what would you not need from God that you do now? Or what would you need that you also need now?

....

We're all children of *Our Father in heaven*. Some of us, though, may have difficulty calling God *Father*. Maybe we have had painful dealings with dads. Not every male does the role of father justice. Still, human beings have a wide range of experiences with moms, dads, coaches, teachers, mentors, the whole set of persons of whom we might say, "Although God is spirit, God's nature is like that of a mom or dad or coach or teacher or mentor." Rather than poll our experience, maybe it would be helpful to remember from whence Jesus was coming.

In biblical times, as in all times, mothers valued their children. Isaiah 66: 13 records God as saying, *"As a mother comforts her child, so I'll comfort you."* (M) Still, in the culture of the biblical world, women were rarely granted the power that men had to provide for their families. Widows and orphans had virtually no rights or protection. Calling God *Mother* in such a situation would not have described God's ability to provide for our needs.

Jesus did not devalue women. In the gospels he heals, saves, befriends, and teaches women just as he did men. He held in high esteem the five women in his genealogy – Tamar, Rahab, Ruth, Bathsheba, and Mary, persons who relied on God in dire circumstances, women whose faithfulness was as great if not greater than that of any male. Other ancient civilizations did not even mention women in genealogies. His did.

According to the Gospel of John, Jesus was on the cross near death when the following transaction occurred:

When Jesus saw his mother and the disciple whom he loved standing beside her, he said to his mother, "Woman, here is your son." Then he said to the disciple, "Here is your mother." And from that hour the disciple took her into his own home. John 19: 26-27 (NRSV)

In a society that did not have a social security system, provision needed to be made for the support of his mom. *Honor your father and your mother,* Commandment 5.

The Creation story in Genesis 2 says that Eve was taken from Adam's rib to be loved as a person of equal stature and dignity, the two of them joined at the rib, standing side by side, rather than taken from his heel to be crushed underfoot. This belief, though, had not become an economic or civil rights reality in Jesus' day. Even though both mothers and fathers valued their children, it was the men, not the women, who had the power to make an adequate living, command justice, and provide for their children.

The God in heaven who values and provides for all human beings is spirit. In the Bible, God is called Lord, Creator, Almighty, etc. All these words tell us something valid about God's nature. But the one word that best describes God's nature, according to Jesus, is *Father.*

24

Question:

16. What doesn't work for you about calling God *Father*? What name do you prefer? Is there another name that connotes "values us" and "provides for us"?

. . . .

In Heaven

Heaven is the new world coming, the biblical kingdom of *heaven*, the culmination of Jesus' work. But it's also the realm of the unseen, the spiritual world as opposed to the material, the eternal as opposed to the ephemeral, the realm where God, who is spirit, dwells and reigns fully even now.

As such, heaven is foundational for quality of life today. The spiritual connections taught and exemplified by Jesus – to God, self, others, creation, peoples – gives shape to how I behave in the material world. On earth, we are all children of Our Father *in heaven*, Ourins. There is no one else in my neighborhood.

Some people are of the opinion that simply being human ought to be reason enough to treat each other with respect. I agree; still, I have additional reason. I believe in God Our Father *in heaven*.

People say, "*In heaven*, I'll be with all my loved ones." More to the point, *in heaven* we'll love all who are there. Jesus, in TLP, provides me the foundation to begin such a life now.

Tony Campolo tells a story of what happened in Moscow when WWII came to an end. Russia lost forty million people during the war. Every family was affected. Fueled by this hatred, the citizens of Moscow lined the street and shouted obscenities at the German soldiers, who had been released from the city jail to march to the train station and be sent home.

First came the officers, who had fared rather well compared to the other prisoners. They marched in goose-step fashion, showing that their imprisonment had not broken their spirit. It was all the police could do to keep the citizens from breaking through their lines and tearing the soldiers apart.

But then came silence as the crowd noticed who came next, the enlisted men. They had not fared so well. They were skin and bones, dressed in rags. They didn't march in goose-step fashion. It was all they could do to drag themselves along the street.

The silence was broken when a woman broke through the lines and gave one of the soldiers a piece of bread. The crowd then followed her example, person after person breaking through to give food to the German enlisted men.

The German soldier who told Tony Campolo this story said, "I couldn't believe it. It was like they recognized we weren't the enemy. We were just someone's little boy, sick and dying, far away from home." (2)

Question:

17. Given that most people tend to be okay with the Usins in their neighborhoods, but not the Urins, how does Jesus solve this problem? We are all of us what?

. . . .

A motorcycle shop across town hands out business cards, "If Jesus lived today, he'd ride a Harley." Librarians for Christ send out notices, "If Jesus were here today, which your book is not, he would tell us a story." Equestrians for Christ brand their business cards with, "If Christ was teaching today, he'd give the Sermon on His Mount."

Our Father in heaven produces yet another card. "If Jesus was sitting at the table, he'd cut the cards in favor of everyone."

When I pray the words Our Father in Heaven,

God is able to search my life and bring to mind instances in which I have not treated persons as though they are also God's children. I owe God better.

...I may be reminded of politicians who want my vote, yet who enthusiastically divide the messy world of Ourins into one of Usins and Urins. But isn't insanity voting election after election for an approach that doesn't work for the common good?

...I may be reminded of corporations that claim they are concerned about the public wellbeing; yet, they treat their lower-level employees horribly, and/or lie about how their manufacturing processes are not damaging the environment, and/or cause the economy to tank due to their greed, and, in spite of being a public blight, still make obscene profits. How concerned, then, should I be that I purchase their products or services?

...I may be prompted to think about the difficulty posed by certain people in the neighborhood. Neighbors can be uncooperative, even dangerous at times, not at all interested in the common good. I need Our Father's guidance when it comes to how I think about such persons and how I interact with them. Jesus never said that being his follower was going to be easy. Still, my

27

starting point is to treat all others as I'd want to be treated. And this can make a big difference in dealing with difficult people.

...I also may be prompted to question if God really does exist and if *Our Father* is God's nature. Atheists may be surprised by what goes on in the heads and hearts of believers, but why? God's address is *in heaven*, which doesn't even appear on Google Maps. And let's be real. Who doesn't at times have doubts? Doubts are part and parcel of one's faith. As Flannery O'Conner once said, *"When we get our spiritual house in order, we'll be dead. Doubt goes on. You arrive at enough certainty to make your way, but it is making it in darkness. Don't expect faith to clear things up for you. Trust not certainty."*

Doubts can't be ignored. God's presence and nature obviously cannot be proven in a court of law, but I have witnessed instance after instance in which persons treat others as they themselves would want to be treated. I've seen people help total strangers as though these people are their neighbors, and do so at a cost. I've seen people not discriminate against others, when their own family or friends would certainly have done so, and then suffer recriminations for their actions. And when I see such persons carrying on Our Father's work, it's enough. I'm grateful to live in a material world into which such eternal values have seeped, are seeping, and will continue to break out in human behavior. Jesus offers a better way of living with one another that we so often settle for.

5

Hallow Your Name (Petition 1)

The King James Bible translates the first petition as, *Hallowed be thy name*. The Jerusalem Bible, *May your name be held holy*. The Message, *Reveal who you are*.

Because all six of the petitions of The Lord's Prayer are in the imperative mood, the language of exhortation, I prefer *Hallow your name*, the literal rendering of the Greek text. *Reveal who you are* is also good. And to *hallow* is to reveal as *holy*.

Such encouragement is consistent with God's nature. I'm not urging Our Father to do anything that God isn't already doing. I'm rooting for God to continue. I'm pledging my support. *"Go for it, God! I'm with you and I'm for you! Hallow your name!"*

In the Biblical era, one's name revealed one's nature. When God *hallows* his name, God's nature is ultimately revealed as holy, meaning different from and greater than all other powers, in a class by itself. No other power holds humankind in such esteem. Power by no other name adequately provides Our needs.

When I pray, *"Hallow your name"*, I am lamenting the reality that many do not know God. I call on God to continue revealing both his existence and nature so that others might also have the opportunity to know God Our Father.

Hallow is not a much-used word. Apart from TLP and *Harry Potter and the Deathly Hallows,* many would never hear the word *hallow* other than on Halloween. I, myself, don't often use the word in daily conversation. Still, it's not like there are no *hallowing*-like activities.

From time to time persons make the claim that a person or a team or a band is greater than other persons or teams or bands. When I taught high school in the early 1980s, my students wore T-shirts that touted their favorite music groups – "Judas Priest Rules!" or "Prince Rules!" or "Bon Jovi Rules!" In response I made my own, "Buddy Holly Rules!" *Hallow your name* is like saying, *"Our Father, let it be known that you rule!"*

The giving of credits for a TV show or movie is also a sort of *hallowing* using a list. The actor or actress with the most clout is listed first. Those with lesser clout are listed below. When I pray *"Hallow your name"*, I'm saying, *"Reveal who you are, Our Father, so that on the marquee of life you will receive top billing!"*

Questions:

18. In the movie, *The Tao of Steve,* Dex says around a campfire that romantic love is the chief religion of America. We give our significant other more attention than we give to our relationship to God. When his friend protests that people pray to God all the time, Dex says it's only to grovel or get something. He claims that his prayers to God are more of the sort, "How was your day, God?" or "Did you catch Letterman last night?" Some sons and daughters do not give their parents encouragement. They may think of the parent in terms of being grownup and capable and having no need of such support. The six petitions of TLP are in the imperative mood. Do you think that God likes to hear us say, "Go for it, God! I'm with you and I'm for you!" And do you have a need to express such support?

19. The Ten Commandments, Exodus 20: 1-17, begins with a commandment that hallows God's name. *You shall have no other gods before me* (or beside me or in addition to me). In a world filled with gods or powers, no other powers are as important to us as is Our Father in heaven. What powers do you have difficulty keeping in their place?

·······

Kids in my religion classes used to say that Pharoah was a powerful dude. Not only did he *walk like an Egyptian,* but no one hassled him, not even INS about his enslaving undocumented Israelites. God hassled him, though, and sent Moses to tell him to let the Israelite slaves go.

 Pharoah said, "Who is the Lord, that I should obey him and let Israel go? I do not know the Lord, and I will not let Israel go." Exodus 5:2 (NIV)

 Pharoah did not *hallow* Gods name, did not honor and obey the Lord, because he did not know the Lord. He probably knew that his Israelite slaves worshiped some god or another. Who didn't? A tribe that lived along the Mediterranean Ocean, the Surfers, worshiped the sun god Ray, praying for a tan that would win the George Hamilton Bronze Age Invitational. The Dinnerite tribe of Canaan worshiped the god Baal, gathering every night for fellowship dinners at the Taco Baal. And the sheep-herding Roswellites worshiped a strange disc that had fallen from the sky bringing them tourism business.

 Pharoah did not know the Lord because God had not revealed himself to Pharoah as he had to Moses. Thus, a hallowing follows.

31

Right off the bat, Moses tells Pharoah God's name. But what happens before Pharoah knows the power behind the name? The Ten Plagues. Agreeing to let the Israelites leave Egypt. Going back on this decision. Pharoah's army drowning in the Red Sea. It would have gone so much better had Pharoah come to an Aha moment earlier as opposed to later. All this in Exodus 5-14.

There are many today who would say they have had no real experience of Our Father. They may have heard of the God of Jesus, but they'd never say, "Alex, I'll take 'Our Father in Heaven' for a true daily double." *Hallow your name* is a prayer that they come to know of God's existence and nature as Our Father reveals it to them.

Questions:

20. How do you express the honor in which someone or something is held? In your experience, to what persons, entities, or powers do people give ultimate allegiance? Mixed allegiance?

21. In what ways do you think Our Father is different from and greater than all other powers? You might think also of God's other names.

22. What does "One nation under God" say to you about the loyalty owed to Uncle Sam versus loyalty owed to Our Father? Why is there a disconnect between what many Christians believe and how they behave in the public sphere?

23. The Gospel of Matthew ends like this. *And Jesus came and said to them, "All authority in heaven and on earth has been*

given to me. Go therefore, and make disciples of all nations,
baptizing them in the name of the Father and of the Son and of
the Holy Spirit, and teaching them to obey everything that I
have commanded you. And remember, I am with you always, to
the end of the age." Matthew 28:18-20 (NRSV)

Do you think that "make disciples of all nations" means make
everyone in every place a follower of Jesus? Or does it mean go
into all the world and in place after place make disciples, as
many as will? In either case, might not the quality of life in the
neighborhood benefit?

．．．．．．．

When I pray Hallow your name,

at times I have to come clean. Do I truly believe that Our
Father is the most powerful force in the world and in my life?
Many of the people I know say that God is most powerful, but too
often don't act like it.

Instead we give our devotion to other gods. We link our value
to Money or Career Success or Sexual allure or I.Q. or Athletic
Prowess and seek more of whatever these gods provide, in the
hopes that we will become more valuable. We don't question our
devotion to and reliance upon the various powers in our lives. Our
Father often places way down the list.

There are many names of power in our world in addition to
those mentioned above – Multi-national Corporations, Uncle Sam,
the Stock Market, Technology, Violence, Propaganda, University,
the Media – the list goes on and on. And these names are powerful.
When I do not question what these powers ask of me or offer me or
the damage they do to others, they can command my allegiance,
loyalty that belongs to the true God. For when I pray *"Hallow your*

33

name", I'm also saying that my primary allegiance belongs to Our Father. I owe God a lifestyle appropriate for a follower of Jesus, not just any sort of lifestyle.

On the other hand, when I pray, *"Hallow your name,"* I think of how powerful the name is when it comes to the wellbeing of humankind. That the God who created it all, the Creator, and the God to whom we owe our ultimate allegiance, the Lord; that the nature of this God is Our Father, the one who values and provides for each and every human being as the best of parents do for their children, then I can think of no greater God.

6

Your Kingdom Come (Petition 2)

First words can be important. Upon setting foot on the moon, Neil Armstrong said, "One small step for man, one giant leap for mankind." Jesus said upon beginning his public ministry, *"Turn away from your sins, because the Kingdom of heaven is near!"* Matthew 4: 17 (GNB)

The good news is that Our Father's rule of this life has arrived. Jesus inaugurated God's kingdom and invites all to live within it. But this rule is not present fully, only partially. We have glimpses of heaven on earth, for God's kingdom breaks in gloriously on occasion, but there is much more to come.

The fullness of God's rule is the concern of Petition 2. I pray *"Your kingdom come!"* in the imperative mood or in the sense of *Make your kingdom come!* And I do so to lament the way things are today – the world largely rejects God's rule – and to call on God to complete the work begun by Jesus. *Bring the world fully within Your rule!*

Your kingdom come reminds me that this life is not yet how God intends it to be. God is still at work putting all things right. I look forward to the time when there is justice and peace and an equitable distribution of life's goods. And I do so knowing that the completion of God's rule will take place on God's timetable, no one else's. *The day of the Lord will come like a thief in the night.* 1 Thessalonians 5: 2. (NRSV)

The Apostles' Creed, which is recited in many worship services, looks forward to the arrival of God's kingdom in its fullness. It says the following:

I believe in God, the Father Almighty, maker of heaven and earth; and in Jesus Christ his only Son, our Lord; who was conceived by the Holy Spirit, born of the Virgin Mary, suffered under Pontius Pilate, was crucified, dead and buried; the third day he rose from the dead; he ascended into heaven, and sits on the right hand of God the Father, *from whence he shall come to judge the quick and the dead.* I believe in the Holy Spirit, the Holy Catholic Church, the communion of saints, the forgiveness of sins, the resurrection of the body, and the life everlasting. Amen.

This creed contains a summary of how God has been at work, is at work, and will be at work in the world. God made all that there is. God is responsible for the birth and ministry of Jesus. Jesus was crucified, yet God raised him from the dead as a vindication of his life and message. He ascended into heaven and rules with God. In his physical absence, the church, guided and enlivened by the Holy Spirit, carries on his work until the end of time as we know it. Then the quick, or living, and the dead will be raised to judgment, which marks the beginning of life in the fullness of the kingdom of God.

Remember the alienations and estrangements caused by sin in Chapter 3? All of this will be put right once again in the fullness of God's rule, meaning our relationships to God, to self, to others, to creation, and peoples with peoples. The following are among several passages of scripture that witness that this is the case.

Paul says about the unpredicted arrival of God's kingdom:

36

We will not all die, but we will all be changed, in a moment, in the twinkling of an eye, at the last trumpet. For the trumpet will sound, and the dead will be raised imperishable, and we will be changed. For this perishable body must put on imperishability, and this mortal body must put on immortality. 1 Corinthians 15:51-53 (NRSV)

Rather than being a disembodied spirit in the kingdom of heaven, I have the hope of being changed into a new and improved body, as was Jesus; yet, one not totally unlike what I have now. After his resurrection Jesus appeared to the disciples in his new body.

While they were talking about this, Jesus himself stood among them and said to them, "Peace be with you." They were startled and terrified, and thought that they were seeing a ghost. He said to them, "Why are you frightened, and why do doubts arise in your hearts? Look at my hands and my feet; see that it is I myself. Touch me and see; for a ghost does not have flesh and bones as you see that I have." And when he had said this, he showed them his hands and his feet. While in their joy they were disbelieving and still wondering, he said to them, "Have you anything here to eat?" They gave him a piece of fish, and he took it and ate in their presence." Luke 24: 36-43 (NRSV)

In a post-resurrection body, I have nothing of which be ashamed. This body will not get sick, break down, or wear out. Weight gain won't be a problem either. Instead of broiled fish, Jesus could have asked for a couple of donuts and a venti mocha without gaining an ounce. (But maybe I'm reading too much into

this. It could be that I actually want to eat in a healthy manner.)
There will be bodily pleasures in the fullness of God's kingdom, as
well as new challenges, tasks, and adventures; purpose that gives
our resurrected lives meaning like we've never experienced before.
I will be right with God and self.

How about creation? In the Book of Revelation, John, the author,
has a vision of the arrival of God's rule in its fullness. A vision, of
course, means what it means rather than what it says, and the
following is a great statement of the hope that Jesus gives me when
I pray *Your kingdom come.*

*Then I saw a new heaven and a new earth, for the first heaven
and the first earth had passed away, and there was no longer any
sea. I saw the Holy City, the new Jerusalem, coming down out of
heaven from God, prepared as a bride beautifully dressed for her
husband. And I heard a loud voice coming from the throne saying,
"Now the dwelling of God is with men, and he will live with them.
They will be his people, and God himself will be with them and be
their God. He will wipe every tear from their eyes. There will be no
more death or mourning or crying or pain, for the old order of
things has passed away."* Revelation 21: 1-4 (NIV)

There is a new creation, a new heaven and earth, that will also
have some degree of continuity with creation as we now know it.
Still, it will be radically better.

*Then the angel showed me the river of the water of life, bright
as crystal, flowing from the throne of God and of the Lamb through
the middle of the street of the city. On either side of the river is the*

*tree of life with its twelve kinds of fruit, producing its fruit each
month; and the leaves of the tree are for the healing of the nations.
Nothing accursed will be found there anymore.* Rev. 22: 1-3a
(NRSV)

A river of water issuing from God's throne, as well as trees and
fruit. What does the river, tree, and fruit remind me of? The Garden
of Eden. What the author of the Book of Revelation anticipates is
Paradise regained, a creation that is not cursed by humankind's sin.
I will be right with God, self, and creation.

What about my estrangement with other people? Scripture quoted
above says, *"There will be no more death or mourning or crying or
pain, for the old order of things has passed away."* That sounds
like an answer to Rodney King's prayer. So does, *Now the dwelling
of God is with men, and he will live with them.*
I also like how life in the city is described.

*The City doesn't need sun or moon for light. God's Glory is its
light, the Lamb its lamp! The nations will walk in its light and
earth's kings bring in their splendor. Its gates will never be shut by
day, and there won't be any night. They'll bring the glory and
honor of the nations into the City. Nothing dirty or defiled will get
into the City, and no one who defiles or deceives.* Revelation 21:
23-27 (M)

Much harm through the ages has been done to persons by other
persons at night. But there is no longer any night. Everything basks
in God's glory. There's no need to shut the city's gates, which is
the first thing to shut when peoples are attacking peoples. Not only

are peoples getting along with peoples in the fullness of God's rule – *The nations will walk in its light and earth's kings bring in their splendor* – but *the leaves of the tree are for the healing of the nations.* I look forward to a time when I'm right with God, self, others, creation, and all peoples. Sounds like number one on anyone's list of the "Top Ten Places to Live".

Questions:

24. One of the criticisms of Jesus by some is this: if he was the Messiah, God's anointed, he would have fully instituted God's rule. There would be no waiting around for more. The kingdom of heaven would have been here at that point. Does this criticism seem valid to you? Why or why not?

25. In Revelation 21:1-4 (above) God moves in at the end of time with humankind in a newly created heaven and earth (combo?), one not totally unlike the earth presently – water, trees, fruit. Do you think it matters what we give God to work with in this new creation? Is it important that we take care of the earth in the meantime? Or can we just trash it?

26. Jesus has a new body in Luke 24: 36-43 (above) following his resurrection from the dead. If we also have this imperishable, immortal body after our resurrection, what do you think talent shows will be like?

When I pray Your kingdom come,

in spite of the enticing visions and teachings of the New Testament, I sometimes wonder if I hadn't rather pray, "Make your kingdom come, but not quite yet." It's not that I don't like the life I have. I have more than enough to eat, whereas more than 800 million of the world's people don't have enough to maintain their health. That translates to one in eight going to bed hungry. I have heating in my home in the winter and AC in the summer. Many don't have access to either and the summers are only going to get hotter. I have clean tap water. My wife doesn't have to lug a jug to a muddy, disease-infested, watering hole two miles away. I've had all sorts of opportunities and experiences.

So, yes, I have it easy in comparison. But Jesus clearly took a stand for the poor or powerless, not the powerful. We're all in this thing together. I owe it to God to pray for and to be of help to all his children. But what kind of help can I be? Small groups of Usins are attempting to make gains everywhere. They're seeing to it that groups of Urins, even though they're growing larger, become even less powerful, have an even smaller portion of life's goods. To even bring up the notion of Ourins is to be drowned out by those Usins in power.

Or is it? Given the illegitimate takeover of the world by Usins – every square inch of planet earth belongs to God – "Make your kingdom come, but not quite yet" is not appropriate. Rather, I pray with confidence in what God can and will do yet, *"Make your kingdom come, now! Complete the rule that Jesus began!"*

7

Your Will Be Done (Petition 3)

In the first two petitions, *Hallow your name* and *Your kingdom come*, to be emphasized is the word *YOUR*. It's God's power and God's rule, no one else's. Because it is, I also pray, *"Your will be done."* I lament how the ways of the world are so often substituted for God's will and encourage Our Father to accept no way but his own.

Imagine a college coach who has labored to build up an athletic program. This head coach is a person of integrity, scrupulously observing the rules that govern his sport. But one day an investigative reporter breaks the story that an assistant coach, along with a group of boosters, have broken the rules in order to recruit sought-after high school players. They have bribed principals to change grades on transcripts, and they have paid athletes under the table. The head coach is devastated. He had no idea this was going on. He would never have approved. Not only has his program been derailed, but his name has been tarnished.

"But we won!" say the boosters.

"But we cheated," says the coach.

Because good intentions aren't the same as God's will, I can likewise tarnish Our Father's name. What might seemingly work in a given situation may not at all be an appropriate reflection upon God's character. If the answer on *Jeopardy* is, "Be untrue to his nature," the question is, "What one thing can Our Father not do?"

That the end may not justify the mean is also the issue in Jesus' third temptation.

Again the devil took him to a very high mountain and showed him all the kingdoms of the world and their splendor.
"All this I will give you," he said, "if you will bow down and worship me." Matthew 4: 8,9 (NIV)

Satan displays his stock of techniques and resources in the hope that Jesus will equip himself with them. This temptation isn't the devil saying, "Abandon the work God has given you." This is the devil saying, "Why not use my means to do God's work? My ways get results."

Satan is deviously asking Jesus to buy in to the thinking that the end justifies any mean. But Our Father's isn't just any rule or kingdom.

"Away with you, Satan! for it is written, 'Worship the Lord your God and serve only him.'" Matthew 4:10 (NRSV)

Trying to establish God's kingdom by the use of worldly ways is the same as serving two masters, not one. And Jesus says elsewhere that *You cannot worship two gods at once.* Matthew 6:24 (M) Yielding to this temptation would result in furthering Satan's influence at the expense of misrepresenting Our Father.

Even the best of intentions can lead to behaviors that do not hallow God's name or contribute to the fullness of God's rule. Such techniques are not true to God's nature. Thus, I pray, *"Your will be done! Accept no way but yours!"*

Questions:

27. Inappropriate means of furthering God's rule include the use of pressure to the end that a person adopt a certain belief or convert to Christianity. What examples of this have you experienced? On the other hand, inappropriate means also include watering down what is expected of a follower of Christ? Have you experienced this?

28. Is there ever a situation in which the end justifies any mean? Say waterboarding a suspected terrorist in order to get information? How about going along with an unethical or illegal directive from one's employer when one needs the job?

29. Do you agree with the following? "Followers of Jesus should always be dubious allies of any political party or special interest group or clique. Ours is not to follow the party line blindly, as happened with much of the church in Germany under Hitler. Jesus is Lord of the conscience, the One to whom a follower of Jesus is answerable."

....

Exodus 20: 3-17 contains a list of the Ten Commandments. In the minds of some, *commandments* appear to be fuddy-duddyisms, prohibitions that enslave them to yesteryear's ways of thinking and behaving. Were they free from these commandments, they'd have a great life. Right? (Actually, many are free from the Ten Commandments because, as shown in the past on both Letterman and Leno, most people on the street only know one and one-half commandments.)

Appearances can be deceiving. In the preface to the Ten Commandments, God does not say, *"I am the Lord your God, the*

44

One who rains on your parade." God says, *"I am the Lord your God, who brought you out of the land of Egypt, out of the house of slavery"*? Exodus 20:2 (NRSV) In other words, the Ten Commandments is one of the means God uses to free us from powers that would enslave us, including our own wants and fears, and to put us right with God.

TLP functions in a similar way. As I pray it day after day, God uses it to free me from all that does not seek the good of humankind and creation and to put me right with God, self, others, peoples, and creation.

Jesus begins the Sermon on the Mount with what we call The Beatitudes, Matthew 5: 1-12, statements such as, *Blessed are the pure in heart, for they will see God. Blessed* is a word that tends to underwhelm. Whereas *commandment* can carry a negative connotation, *blessed* is a word that has been so overused it doesn't necessarily mean much anything. Onlookers say, "God bless you!" when I sneeze. People hang up the phone after a conversation saying, "God bless." I'm urged to count my many blessings, referring to the accumulation of possessions that Jesus warns can lead me astray and ruin my life.

On occasion, a person may know exactly what she means when she uses the word, in some instances maybe happy or fortunate. But whatever a person might mean, Jesus used the word *blessed* like a road sign. If scripture is thought of as the roadmap to living with skill as Our Father's children, the beatitudes let us know that we're on the right path.

For example, pure in heart (or motive) means that I act out of a desire for only one thing, God's goodness. Martin Luther King, Jr. said, "Cowardice asks the question, is it safe? Expediency asks the question, is it politic. Vanity asks the question, is it popular? But conscience asks the question, is it right?"

To ask and act upon any of the questions above, other than the last one, is to be impure of heart or motive.

TLP functions in a similar way to the Beatitudes. It orients me so that I'm headed in the right direction, puts me right with God again and again.

Question:

30. *"Blessed are the meek, for they will inherit the earth,"* is one of the Beatitudes. How do you understand the word *meek*? Most understand *meek* as does J. Upton Dickson, a humorist who has built a comedy routine around the word. He even wrote a brochure called *Cower Power* and has founded a group of submissive, spineless people called DOORMATS, "Dependent Organization of Really Meek and Timid Souls." Their motto is: "The meek shall inherit the earth – if that's okay with everyone else." Their symbol is a yellow traffic light.

Still, just as *blessed* and *commandment* can mean other than many think, so can the New Testament Greek word praus, here translated meek. As Jesus uses this word, it refers to the gentle and considerate, yes, but the gentle and considerate who reject the power-hungry, aggressive, violent ways of the world. These people are even willing to use peaceful means to stand up to the intimidation of those who throw their weight around. Defined in this manner, the meek include some of the bravest people who have ever lived as they peacefully oppose hatred and intimidation. Because they do, the future belongs to them as opposed to those who try to take the earth by force.

46

Which understanding of *meek* do you think is the better response to *"Your will be done"*?

31. Do you know persons who confront the intimidation of others non-violently?

....

When I pray Your will be done,
I wish I had Jesus' resolve. For when I am tempted, too often I'm like W.C. Fields. I look for loopholes. I can rationalize with the best of them, and it is sometimes easier to ask forgiveness than permission. In a success oriented society, such as ours, the ways of the world that are currently getting results are certainly tempting. But always at the expense of integrity, peace, justice, and the wellbeing of Urins.

8

On earth as it is in heaven (The First Qualifier)

On earth as it is in heaven qualifies petitions 1-3, *Hallow your name, Your kingdom come, Your will be done.*

I pray for it be revealed *on earth* that not only does God exist, but that Our Father's power is above and beyond all other powers. God values each and every human being as the best of fathers loves his children and provides for our needs (petition 1). I pray for the completion of God's rule *on earth*, the kingdom inaugurated by Jesus (petition 2). And I pray that the means of bringing about Our Father's rule *on earth* be consistent with God's will, as opposed to the ways of the world (petition 3).

In the spiritual world that is foundational to the material world, all of the above is apparent – Our Father's name is above all else, God rules, and all freely choose to do it Our Father's way. In the kingdom of heaven that is to come fully, and that will break in to this world gloriously at times until then, this will also be the case.

9

Give Us This Day Our Daily Bread (Petition 4)

In petition 1, *Hallow your name*, I lament the reality that Our Father is not known by all his children. I pray for God to reveal his nature so that others might have the opportunity to know Our Father.

One way I'm supportive of God in this revelation is by being content with what God provides. I even vow in petition 4 that enough is enough by praying as a member of Jesus' church, *"I'm with you, Our Father! Give us this day our daily bread. I need no more!"*

God gives what I need to live fully as his child, one who reflects Our Father's nature and helps carry out Our Father's interests. I have enough. Too often, though, I fear that I need more than God provides – more courage, more protection, more faith, more hope, etc. But I don't. And I'm not right with God when I expect more than is needed before doing or saying the right thing. I owe God better than to act as though I'm not valued and my needs aren't being provided. Rather than go about my life as though I have inadequate resources, I pray, *"Give me bread, that which fuels life as your child, sufficient for the day. Enough is enough."*

Those who do not know *Our Father* can gain an acquaintance through the behavior of Jesus' followers. In the New Testament Letter of 1 Peter, it is said that I've done a good job in this regard if either of two things happens: one, a person says to me or thinks of me, "I don't know why you do the things you do, but I'm glad you're my neighbor." Or two, "I don't know why you do the things you do. Would you explain it to me?"

Neither of these two questions can occur if I behave as though Our Father doesn't value me. Nor can they happen if my behavior implies that I want more than God provides.

In the Greek of TLP, Jesus says, *Give us our bread for tomorrow today – Ton arton hemon ton epiousion dos hemin semaron.*

Stated this way, I am pointed to Exodus 16, a story in which the Israelites do not trust that God will provide enough in the wilderness. They complain:

"If only we had died by the hand of the Lord in the land of Egypt, when we sat by the fleshpots and ate our fill of bread; for you have brought us out into this wilderness to kill this whole assembly with hunger." Exodus 16: 3 (NRSV)

But what happens? God rains bread (manna) in the morning that the people cook for their evening meal. There is enough to sustain them on their journey. Since the Hebrews measured their days from sundown to sundown, God provides bread for tomorrow (eaten after sundown), but bread one gathers today (in the morning), exactly the way it is stated in the Greek of TLP, *Give us our bread for tomorrow today.* Still, some have their doubts.

When the Israelites saw it, they said to each other, "What is it?" For they did not know what it was.

Moses said to them, "It is the bread the Lord has given you to eat. This is what the Lord has commanded: Each one is to gather as much as he needs. Take an omer for each person you have in your tent."

The Israelites did as they were told; some gathered much, some little. And when they measured it by the omer, he who gathered much did not have too much, and he who gathered little did not have too little. Each one gathered as much as he needed.

"Then Moses said to them, "No one is to keep any of it until morning."

However, some of them paid no attention to Moses; they kept part of it until morning, but it was full of maggots and began to smell. So Moses was angry with them. Exodus 16: 15-20 (NIV)

God provides enough of what I need to live as his child. Exodus 16 teaches me that wanting more before taking the next step of faith puts me at odds with God. And Jesus teaches me that if I pray for Our Father to hallow his name, my task is to live as though I'm valued and my needs provided.

I obviously think that the bread Our Father provides in TLP is spiritual bread. Why spiritual rather than whole wheat? Elsewhere Jesus says about Our Father's giving nature:

So do not worry, saying, "What shall we eat?" or "What shall we drink?" or "What shall we wear?" For the pagans run after all these things, and your heavenly Father knows that you need them. But seek first his kingdom and his righteousness, and all these things will be given to you as well. Matthew 6: 31-33 (NIV)

That God provides our material needs is a given according to Jesus. Why would he then teach his followers to pray for whole wheat when he says it's provided? Obviously, not every individual at a particular time has sufficient food, drink, clothing, housing, schooling, and medical attention. Even though God provides enough for all humankind, this sufficiency is not always shared. It can be hoarded, in effect, by those who have way more than enough.

When it comes to having enough of life's goods, humankind faces a distribution problem not of Divine making, one perpetuated by the Usins versus Urins point of view, one that at times is complicated by an unruly creation. It is fitting that Jesus ends the above teaching with, *But seek first his kingdom and his righteousness.* For when I seek God's rule, I value others, share life's goods, and work for enough for all. Sustained by spiritual bread, I work to help overcome the human-made distribution problem involving whole wheat.

Of course, my situation can change in a minute, and I may find myself in need. How many refugees are there in the world who enjoyed a life filled with more than enough until violence chased them off their lands or from their towns? How many were doing okay until their homes were flooded or destroyed by an earthquake? How many people had a decent standard of living until they came down with a disabling illness or were overwhelmed by debt having to do with an uninsured illness? How many workers have lost good jobs that aren't coming back? *"Do not boast about tomorrow, for you do not know what a day may bring."* Proverbs 27:1

Working to end this manmade, Usin/Urin distribution problem is also the concern of another of Jesus' teachings:

When the Son of Man comes in his glory, and all the angels with him, he will sit on his throne in heavenly glory. All the nations will be gathered before him, and he will separate the people one from another as a shepherd separates the sheep from the goats. He will put the sheep at his right hand and the goats at the left.

Then the King will say to those on his right, "Come, you who are blessed by my Father; take your inheritance, the kingdom prepared for you since the creation of the world. For I was hungry and you gave me something to eat, I was thirsty and you gave me something to drink, I was a stranger and you invited me in, I needed clothes and you clothed me, I was sick and you looked after me, I was in prison and you came to visit me."

Then the righteous will answer him, "Lord, when did we see you hungry and feed you, or thirsty and give you something to drink? When did we see you a stranger and invite you in, or needing clothes and clothe you? When did we see you sick or in prison and go to visit you?"

The king will reply, "I tell you the truth, whatever you did for one of the least of these brothers of mine, you did it to me." Mt. 25: 31-40 (NIV)

In the Bible, the poor are those who do not have the power to fend for themselves. The poor are powerless in the sense that they presently do not have access to that which provides them with enough of life's goods. This can be long-term or for a shorter duration. But because charity is justice for the poor, *daily bread* in TLP fuels generosity. *"Give us this day generosity so we might share with those in need."* Or because many live according to the false golden rule, "Those who have the gold make the rule," daily bread may fuel the daring to take a stand on behalf of the powerless. *"Give us this day courage with which to seek fairness."* Or because too often no good deed goes unpunished, *"Give us this day the endurance to put up with the abuse."*

If I was in a tight, I'd certainly pray for a job or food or housing or health care or access to needed education or whatever was needed. Still, whole wheat isn't what Jesus means by bread in TLP. It is bread of another sort, spiritual food.

Jesus clarifies the sort of daily bread that is most needed in the first of his three temptations, this when Satan tempts him to prove that he is God's Son by taking his material needs into his own hands.

"Then Jesus was led by the Spirit into the desert to be tempted by the devil. After fasting forty days and forty nights, he was hungry. The tempter came to him and said, 'If you are the Son of God, tell these stones to become bread.'

"Jesus answered, 'It is written: Man does not live on bread alone, but by every word that comes from the mouth of God.'" Mt. 4: 1-4 (NIV)

Life as God's children is sustained by more than just whole wheat. It is fueled by the commandments and promises of Our Father in heaven. The proof that Jesus is God's Son is not that he can turn stones into loaves of bread, but that he relies first and foremost on spiritual daily bread, *every word that comes from the mouth of God.* These promises and commandments strengthen Jesus for a life of obedience, including the trust that his physical needs will be met in due time. *Then the devil left him, and angels came and attended him.* Mt. 4: 11.

Questions:

32. Christians sometimes give as their reason for going to worship, "the need to be fed." How do you understand this statement?

33. If everyone in the world believed in the God of Jesus, Our Father, and regarded all others as their spiritual brothers and sisters, would there be hunger?

34. What assistance might a person need in order to access enough food, water, health care, housing, clothing, education?

35. Most of us have thought about some task, "I could never do that!" We think we don't have the resources or skill to do the job. Yet, the Bible gives us the following examples: Moses is commanded by God to lead the Israelites out of Egypt. Moses responds by saying that he could never do such a thing. He is a poor speaker. Exodus 4:10.

    Jesus says to the father of an epileptic boy, this regarding his ability to heal, *"All things can be done for the one who believes."* The father cries out, *"I believe help my unbelief!"* Mark 9: 23, 24 (NRSV)

    Abraham and Sarah find God's promise that they will become parents hard to believe. Sarah is too old, can't possibly happen. Such a notion is laughable. Genesis 18: 9-15. Yet, Moses leads the Israelites out of Egyptian slavery, the father's son is healed, and Sarah bears Isaac. Have you ever been surprised by having enough of what it took to do the job? Are you willing to see if you have enough?

36. In Matthew 25: 31-40 (above) what reasons do Jesus give for befriending the friendless, visiting the prisoner or the sick, feeding the hungry, giving water to the thirsty, and clothing the ill-clad?

37. Can inordinate praise of the lifestyles of the rich and famous give others the wrong understanding of Our Father's nature? How about the lengths to which we go in an attempt to feel safe and secure?

·······

When I Pray Give us today daily bread,

I remember that I also pray *Hallow your name*, Our Father, the One who values each and every human being, your children, and who provides for Our needs.

My task, then, is to trust that God will take care of my needs, spiritual first and then material. I'm out of line to expect more. My lot in this life is to be content with enough, and not only bear witness that God provides, but help God overcome the Usins (Powerful) versus Urins (Poor) distribution problem. Trusting that God provides enough is essential to being right with God.

10

Forgive Us Our Debts As We Forgive Our Debtors (Petition 5)

Your kingdom come, petition 2, turns my attention to the arrival of God's rule in its fullness. *"Go for it! I'm with you and I'm for you!"* And one way I'm with Our Father is by praying along with others of Jesus' followers, *"Forgive us our debts (sins) as we forgive our debtors (those who owe us better)."*

If my hope is for the fullness of God's rule, I strive to live within God's rule now. But there is no way I can do this apart from God's forgiveness. Those who heard Jesus' Sermon on the Mount in person responded, "We can't live up to these expectations! We ourselves can never be right with God!"

And they were right. Being right with God is a way of life made possible by God's guidance and forgiveness. Our Father persistently takes the initiative in restoring our relationship when I give less than is due, but Our Father does not lower his expectations.

If Jesus commands, *"Love your enemies and pray for those who persecute you,"* Matthew 5:44, God holds me accountable for behavior involving hatred or apathy. Our Father doesn't say, "Oh, you didn't mean it. Forget it this time. It's okay." God doesn't excuse what I have done. God blames but will forgive, which requires that I return to God's way.

Given that I am a recipient of God's forgiveness, as well as one who follows Jesus by striving to reflect Our Father's nature, mine is also to forgive others for giving me less than my due. *Forgive us our debts, as I forgive my debtors*. How great a debt God forgives, in comparison to the damage inflicted against me, is found in Jesus' story about a king settling accounts with his servants:

"For this reason the kingdom of heaven may be compared to a king who wished to settle accounts with his slaves. When he began the reckoning, one who owed him ten thousand talents was brought to him; and, as he could not pay, his lord ordered him to be sold, together with his wife and children and all his possessions, and payment to be made.

"So the slave fell on his knees before him, saying, 'Have patience with me, and I will pay you everything.' And out of pity for him, the lord of that slave released him and forgave him the debt. But that same slave, as he went out, came upon one of his fellow slaves who owed him a hundred denarii, and seizing him by the throat, he said, 'Pay what you owe.'

"Then his fellow slave fell down and pleaded with him, 'Have patience with me, and I will pay you.' But he refused; then he went and threw him into prison until he would pay the debt. When his fellow slaves saw what had happened, they were greatly distressed, and they went and reported to their lord all that had taken place. Then his lord summoned him and said to him, 'You wicked slave! I forgave you all that debt because you pleaded with me. Should you not have had mercy on your fellow slave, as I had mercy on you?'

"And in anger his lord handed him over to be tortured until he would pay his entire debt. So my heavenly Father will also do to every one of you, if you do not forgive your brother or sister from your heart." Matthew 18: 23-35 (NRSV)

A talent was more than fifteen years of wages for a laborer in Jesus' day. Ten thousand talents of silver was more than a laborer could make in one hundred-fifty thousand years. The king's servant earned more than a laborer; still, there was no way he could pay his debt, same Greek word for debt, *opheilama*, as in TLP.

In order that the king recoup some of his money, he orders that the servant and his family be sold to another master. But in response to the man's pleading, the king forgives the debt. The account is settled, the relationship put right. It was expected from then on that the servant give the king his due.

But instead of being thankful and taking his family out to dinner to celebrate, the man bumps into a servant who owes him one hundred denarii, the equivalent of three months wages, and demands payment. When this other fellow asks him to be patient, the servant has him thrown in prison until the debt is paid. The king finds out and is enraged. He then punishes the servant whose debt he had forgiven by locking him in an empty bank vault for 150,000 years, where he has to listen to nothing but The Beatles' recording of *Money*. "The best things in life are free, but you can keep 'em for the birds and bees, now give me money..."

If I desire God's kingdom to come in its fullness, I strive to live within God's rule now. I do this by accepting God's forgiveness and by forgiving others. If the magnitude of my debt to God is 150,000 years of wages, the debt of those who owe me better is oftentimes on the scale of three months' wages. But regardless of how great the damage – and certain offenses obviously run up a greater tab than others – I am being put right with God and others when I pray as a member of Jesus' church, *"Forgive us our debts as we forgive our debtors."*

Listening to people talk about forgiveness is confusing. For example, a woman called in to a radio talk show to say that she had forgiven a fellow who committed a horrible crime. But the crime occurred two-thousand miles away and involved no one she knew. Why forgive? Who has the time, energy, or need? I can be horrified or outraged, but it's all I can do just to forgive those who have hurt my family and me.

I don't seem to have a need to forgive persons responsible for offenses that don't involve me personally. For other than personal offenses, my task is to join with the community in seeking justice if that is what is called for. I may even be impartial enough to sit on a jury. But when a person has harmed me or those closest to me, then I need to forgive, which takes time and energy.

I have heard people say that only wusses forgive others. Offenders don't deserve a break. But how about the one who has been harmed, the one to whom better was owed? Doesn't this person deserve a break? Many people have found that if we don't forgive, we keep replaying the offense in our head. It's like we give the offender permission to keep on causing us grief. Or we resent it, begin to carry a grudge. When this is the case, forgiveness is the wise choice. It helps us get on with our lives.

And how do I know that I've forgiven a person? I feel that I'm on my way when I haven't thought about what the (expletive deleted) child of God did to me for quite some time. But then I wake up one morning upset anew. The pain hasn't gone away, it's just been on vacation. There is more work to be done in order that the debt (sin) be forgiven. And so I once again pray, *Forgive us our debts as I forgive this &#@*%!$.*

What does a relationship look like when a person forgives another? Sometimes the original relationship is changed. A relationship within a family or involving a friend might become more guarded, less spontaneous. Or two long-time coworkers might drift apart. They don't become enemies, they just don't hang out like they used to. And this is okay.

Or the relationship can also return to what it once was. In the movie *Places of the Heart*, Ed Harris plays a fellow who cheats on his wife. She finds out and is hurt. Her response consists of icy stares and cold shoulder. He is genuinely remorseful, but there is no thaw in their relationship until one Sunday morning when they're sitting on a hard pew in church. As the congregation prepares to take communion, without taking her eyes off the minister, the wife reaches over and grasps her husband's hand. And does he let out a sigh of relief!

It seems to me that God has a big advantage when it comes to forgiveness. Our Father can just haul off and forget. *"I am He who blots out your transgressions for my own sake, and I will not remember your sins."* Isaiah 43:25 (NRSV)

I can't do that. Without even trying I can forget names, appointments, and how to work trigonometric identities. But it takes effort to lessen the outrage occasioned by what that (Bleep) did to me. To forgive I have to work with God's help to leave it behind.

In Mt. 18: 21, 22, Peter asked Jesus, *"'Lord, if a person sins against me, how often should I forgive? Seven times?' Jesus said to him, 'Not seven times, but, I tell you seventy times seven.'"* In other words, as many times as the person sins against you.

But what if Peter had asked, *"Lord, if a person sins against me just once, how many times must I attempt to forgive this person before I succeed?"* Might not Jesus also say, *"Not seven times, but seventy times seven"*? A bunch. However many it takes.

Questions:

38. There are those who say, "God loves us as we are, period." Others say, "God loves us as we are, but loves us too much to leave us as we are." What do you think?

39. How do you pray for an enemy? What would you say? Would you include yourself also in the prayer?

40. How do you know when you have or have not yet forgiven a person?

. . . .

The Parable of the Prodigal Father

Then Jesus said, "There was a man who had two sons. The younger of them said to his father, 'Father, give me the share of the property that will belong to me.' So he divided his property between them. A few days later the younger son gathered all he had and traveled to a distant country, and there he squandered his property in dissolute living.

"When he had spent everything, a severe famine took place throughout that country, and he began to be in need. So he went and hired himself out to one of the citizens of that country, who sent him to his fields to feed the pigs. He would gladly have filled himself with the pods that the pigs were eating; and no one gave him anything.

"But when he came to himself he said, 'How many of my father's hired hands have bread enough and to spare, but here I am

dying of hunger! I will get up and go to my father, and I will say to him, "Father, I have sinned against heaven and before you; I am no longer worthy to be called your son; treat me like one of your hired hands." '

"So he set off and went to his father. But while he was still far off, his father saw him and was filled with compassion; he ran and put his arms around him and kissed him. Then the son said to him, 'Father, I have sinned against heaven and before you; I am no longer worthy to be called your son.'

"But the father said to his slaves, 'Quickly, bring out a robe – the best one – and put it on him; put a ring on his finger and sandals on his feet. And get the fatted calf and kill it, and let us eat and celebrate; for this son of mine was dead and is alive again; he was lost and is found!' And they began to celebrate." Luke 15: 11-24 (NRSV)

Over the years words have entered the English language from the French language, including several words of the Christian faith – prophet, saint, Baptist, miracle, paradise, sacrament. Also, French words that have to do with excess – prodigy, prodigious, prodigality, and prodigal. If you are prodigious you may be called a prodigy, meaning that you have ability or talent in excess of others. There is also an excess with prodigality and prodigal. In fact, there are two ways you can be excessive. A prodigal can be excessively wasteful in spending his money, as was the son in the Luke reading above. Or a prodigal can be excessively graceful in giving love, as was the father.

Two things emerge regarding the Parable of the Prodigal Father. One is that no father in the Middle East would put up with such a son. When the son says, "Father, give me my inheritance now," it was the same as saying, "I wish you were dead, Pop." No

63

father would take such disrespect. The second thing was how the father ran to his son when he saw him coming home. In the Middle East, a man's social class determined his pace. Servants had to hurry, but not the well-to-do. That the dad picked up his robes and ran to embrace the son simply was not done.

God is like the prodigal father in this parable, excessively graceful in giving that form of love known as forgiveness. Whenever a person wants to return to Our Father, she doesn't have to have an appointment. Just show up for the celebration.

One of the things that is interesting about this parable is that the Father restores the son to the position in the family that he had before, giving him one of the best robes, a pair of sandals, and a signet ring, with which to sign documents on his father's behalf. It's like the son had never left.

This is not always the case. Yes, God welcomes me home, but oftentimes there are consequences to my actions, consequences that God's commandments and Jesus' teachings were trying to spare me in the first place. If I gamble and lose the rent money – no matter how repentant I am – I may be evicted, out on the street. If I pass up a job offer because it pays less than I'm making now, it's gone no matter how happy I'd have been taking it. If I lose my temper and post something offensive on Facebook, there can be repercussions no matter how much I regret what I did. Even though I have returned to Our Father, there may be consequences to bear.

Question:

41. The son who had been excessively wasteful was surprised by the warm welcome given him by his father. His brother, though, was mad at the father. He'd stayed at home and done

his job while his brother had gone to the big city and wasted a large portion of the family's fortune in loose living. Yet, he had never been honored with a celebration. Do you think he should ask for his inheritance, leave home, and blow it so that in a few months his dad can throw him a party on his return home? Do you identify with the brother?

....

Regret and Resentment

I see lots of baggage on carousels at airports. It's like watching NASCAR. Around and around it goes, bags crashing into each other and even veering off the carousel. But whereas visible baggage is needed on a trip, at times I may carry around unneeded, invisible baggage.

Invisible, emotional baggage comes from all sorts of experiences and relationships. People say, "She has baggage from her first marriage." Or "He's young to have so much baggage."

I hear it all the time. It's like we've had enough experience pushing or pulling baggage carts that we could become bellhops for the Hotel of Life. But it's emotional baggage. And there are different kinds of emotional baggage, but most fall into the two categories of regret or resentment.

Regret is a feeling that can attach to my own misbehavior, failures, and sins. I did something I wish I hadn't. I owed God better. I owed the person better. I owed myself better. I regret it. Resentment, on the other hand, is how I may feel when I've been mistreated or life didn't work out like I hoped. I resent it. He or she or they or God or life itself owed me better. It wasn't my fault.

It is hard to avoid both feelings. Life happens and I feel one or the other. But there is a difference between feeling regretful or resentful for a short while and being burdened with regret and resentment for years.

So, what might I do with regret and resentment other than lug it around? Take it to the dump and get rid of it. It's only getting in the way of having a life. And I know a landfill that will gladly accept it however often I need to visit. Jesus was crucified at Golgotha. And what was Golgotha? A dump. Seems fitting.

And how well does this work? Even better than giving it to the big bird. (Not the one on *Sesame Street*.) How the big bird handles emotional baggage is like this. Say a lady is either wishing she'd never done what she did or she's hating the one who mistreated her, a suitcase by her side filled with regret or resentment, when a big bird sent from God flies up with a copy of a clean slate in its bill, which covers the sin, in case she lost the original. The slate is wiped clean, regardless of whose fault. And then the big bird takes the bag filled with regret or resentment, flies to a secret ocean thousands of miles away, the deepest ocean in the world, and drops the bag, to which heavy stones have been attached, into the water. And as the baggage sinks, up pops a buoy with a sign that says, "No Fishing Allowed."

There's a sign at Golgotha where one leaves baggage. It says, "What's left at Golgotha, stays at Golgotha."

Questions:

42. If forgiveness is another chance to become the people God intends us to be, but we aren't, which makes more sense to you? God saying to himself, "Okay, I'll forgive you. The slate

is clean, our relationship restored. But you've got to lug around the regret and resentment from now on. It'll teach you to make better choices in the future." Or does God say, "Not only do I forgive you, but let's also trash the regret and resentment. Why on earth do you think you need it?" What are the effects of lugging around regret and resentment?

43. How would you explain the difference between regret and resentment, the one hand, and other consequences of sin on the

44. Must regret and resentment always be preceded by a sin?

....

When I pray Forgive us our debts as we forgive our debtors,
I'm reminded that I am but one of Our Father in heaven's children, related to all human beings as their spiritual brother. When I fail to forgive a person who has given me less than my due, I have created a division in God's family that is not mine to make, an Usin vs. Urin.

And just as I owe God better for my sins – and need forgiveness – I also owe God better than to be lugging around regret and resentment. I may have to live with the consequences of some of my debts (sins), but hanging my head in shame or carrying a chip on my shoulder isn't required.

11

Lead us not into temptation (Petition 6)

When I pray *"Your will be done"*, Petition 3, I lament how the ways of the world are so often substituted for God's will and call on God to accept no way but his own. *"Go for it, Our Father! I'm with you and I'm for you!"* And one way I'm with God is by praying as a member of Jesus' church, *"Lead us not into temptation."*

As mentioned in Chapter 1, perhaps the one thing that is most unclear about The Lord's Prayer involves *Lead us not into temptation*, or *peirasmon* in New Testament Greek. Why would we need to pray this way? Is God going to tempt us to sin if we don't? Does God want us to be obedient on the one hand, yet tempt us to be disobedient on the other? What kind of father treats his children this way?

The following from James is insightful. In this passage, "tempt" translates *peirazein*, the verb form of the noun *peirasmon* in TLP.

When tempted, no one should say, "God is tempting me." For God cannot be tempted by evil, nor does he tempt anyone; but each one is tempted when, by his own evil desire, he is dragged away and enticed. Then, after desire has conceived, it gives birth to sin; and sin, when it is full-grown, gives birth to death. James 1: 13-16 (NIV)

Lead us not into temptation is not to be understood in the sense that God would ever tempt me to depart from God's ways. Temptation stems from my own desire as influenced, says James, by the "evil one". The correct understanding of Petition Six is *Don't let us tempt You with what we want.*

The crowds listening to Jesus teach on the mount knew the Exodus story well. In the Septuagint, the Greek-language version of the Hebrew Bible, *peirazein* can be translated as either "test" or "tempt".

The whole Israelite community set out from the Desert of Sin, traveling from place to place as the Lord commanded. They camped at Rephidim, but there was no water for the people to drink. So they quarreled with Moses, and said, "Give us water to drink."

Moses replied, "Why do you quarrel with me? Why do you put the Lord to the test?" (Or "Why do you tempt the Lord?")

But the people were thirsty for water there, and they grumbled against Moses. They said, "Why did you bring us up out of Egypt to make us and our children and livestock die of thirst?"

Then Moses cried out to the Lord, "What am I to do with this people? They are almost ready to stone me."

The Lord answered Moses, "Walk on ahead of the people. Take with you some of the elders of Israel and take in your hand the staff with which you struck the Nile, and go. I will stand there before you by the rock at Horeb. Strike the rock, and water will come out of it for the people to drink."

So Moses did this in the sight of the elders of Israel. And he called the place Massah and Meribah because the Israelites quarreled and because they tested the Lord (or "tempted the Lord"), *saying, "Is the Lord among us or not?"* Exodus 17: 1-7 (NIV)

The Israelites weren't into hydration nearly as much as water-bottle-toting North Americans. Still, the people were thirsty and demanded water. And it wasn't that God was going to refuse them. Their needs would be provided. (Remember Jesus' needs in his temptation?) But the people were so impatient that they committed an offense. Moses named the place of offense Massah, which can mean "Test", as in putting God to the test, or "Tempt", as in tempting God to do it their way.

This sort of temptation can assume the tone, "If you really love me, God, you'll…" Or perhaps there is no prayer ahead of time. I just do it my way, and when things don't work out like I hoped, I expect God to come to the rescue, which is an act of temptation. "If you really love me, God, you'll get me out of this." Or maybe the tone of my prayers is no different from grumbling about what I don't have, as in Exodus 17. Grumbling produces pressure or tempts God to respond to my wants.

Questions:

45. Have you ever embarked on a course of action without prayerfully considering if it's the right thing to do? And then when you got in a jam, expected God to make things work out? How else might you have tempted God?

46. Is it difficult for you to stop and focus on God's will as opposed to what you want to do?

………

"Lead us not into (the act of) temptation" means, "Don't let me tempt you to do it my way with my prayers, assumptions, and expectations." What kind of a person would I be to pray *"Your will be done",* but then expect God to go along with my will? Certainly not one who is right with God.

Another relevant use of *peirazein,* "to tempt" or "to test," is the second temptation of Jesus:

> *Then the devil took him to the holy city and had him stand on the highest point of the temple. "If you are the Son of God," he said, "throw yourself down; for it is written, 'He will command his angels concerning you, and they will lift you up in their hands, so that you will not strike your foot against a stone.'"*
>
> *Jesus answered him, "It is also written, 'Do not put the Lord your God to the test.'"* (Or better, *"Do not tempt the Lord your God,"* else they will pick you up with a spatula.) Matthew 4: 5-7 (NIV)

When I pray Lead us not into Temptation,

I am reminded that I have also prayed, *"Your will be done."* Because I want to be supportive of what God is doing in the world and how Our Father is doing it, I join with other followers of Jesus in praying, *"Lead us not into temptation"* or *"Do not let me tempt you with my wants."* I owe Our Father better.

12

Deliver Us From Evil (The Second Qualifier)

Deliver us from evil qualifies Petitions 4-6, *Give us this day our daily bread, Forgive us our debts as we forgive our debtors, And lead us not into temptation.*

Evil in TLP is that which opposes God's intent for humankind and planet earth. The influence of evil prompts estrangement between humankind and God, between humankind and the created world, among groups of humans, between individuals, and within self. Because *Us* refers to Jesus' church, not humankind in general, that which is evil can influence me to not be content with enough (Petition 4), to not forgive and accept forgiveness (Petition 5), and to tempt God to do it my way (Petition 6).

Jesus does not say in TLP that I am evil or that anyone is evil, other than Satan. He emphatically points out the reality that evil too often is an influence in my life. When it is, Jesus' church cannot say "amen" to my behavior, nor can others outside the church consider me a good neighbor. Because we're all in this thing together, I need to be delivered from the influence of evil and put right with God.

Question:

47. In what ways do you see evil as an influence in daily life? Do you think "evil" is too harsh a word or not?

72

13

Usins and Urins

As a member of the human race, I am but one of a diverse lot, including what is believed about the Divine. Should I pray as a follower of Jesus without remembering this diversity, I've reduced the scope of God's love and blessing. For regardless of my brothers' and sisters' religious beliefs, sexual orientation, country of origin, political party, rap sheet, language, or skin color, Jesus teaches that God's nature is that of Our Father, the One who values all of us and provides for the needs of all.

Fascism is a point of view associated with the Fascisti Party under Mussolini in Italy. Mussolini, of course, wasn't the only one who viewed the world in the Usin and Urin manner. There was Franco in Spain, Stalin in Russia, and Hitler in Germany. There have also been Slobodan Milosevic as Yugoslavia was collapsing, Pol Pot in Cambodia, Osama Bin Laden, and Idi Amin in Uganda, just to name a few. I have no idea how many fascists there are in the world presently, but I do know that all it takes to become a fascist is to believe in this statement. *There are only two kinds of people in the world. Us and those who don't count.* Fascism is Usins and Urins taken to the extreme.

Usins versus Urins is one of the big challenges presently facing humankind, a challenge aided and abetted by advances in technology, propaganda, and false news. It's the name of the game in Washington, D.C., state capitols, and down the block. Three local white high-school boys were thinking about robbing a small family-owned diner. One of the boys talked the other two out of it because the owner reminded him of his grandfather, an Usin. He might fight back and they would have to harm him. Instead, they robbed a grocery store run by a Korean-American family, Urins in their point of view, pistol-whipping the owner in the process.

Jesus points out a better way, Ourins. And because all others count with God, I am often tolerant in my relationships. But because I also count with God, and because I believe Jesus' message to be the truth, I'm also called to live with conviction. Tolerance and conviction characterize my relationships to others.

Tolerance is most fundamentally a form of humility. I often tolerate viewpoints and behaviors that differ from mine because I have no right to throw my weight around. In fact, who am I in comparison to others? In TLP, *Our Father* points out that I'm other people's brother, not their keeper. *Your will be done* reminds me that my way isn't always God's way. And *Forgive us our debts* busts me for all the many times I have not given God his due. Praying TLP keeps me humble.

Still, because I believe the gospel of Jesus to be true, I'm also obliged to exhibit convictions that are helpful rather than harmful to all my neighbors. Such conviction was displayed by Oskar Schindler. Schindler was a Christian who lived under Hitler's brand of fascism. In the movie based on the true story, *Schindler's List* (3), early on he tolerated the views of the Nazis. He ran his factory as they wanted him to. But as time passed his convictions began to determine his behavior. Tolerance is not at all right with God when some of God's children are being treated as though they don't count. Rather than passively watch the extermination of those who did not believe about the Divine as did he, Schindler risked his life to purchase and preserve their lives. Eleven-hundred Jews lived because their names were on his list.

The fundamental of fascism, that there are only two kinds of people in the world, us and those who don't count, is a basic I cannot tolerate. It is as far from the teachings of Jesus as a fundamental can get. Others matter, for they are my brothers and sisters under the Fatherhood of God, regardless of our differences. All are to be treated as I would want to be treated.

This balance of tolerance and conviction is difficult to maintain. People say, "What is true for you may not be true for me. What is right for you may not be right for me." Consequently, my convictions may appear to be an infringement of the rights of others, whose convictions, whatever they are, are considered just as valid as mine.

I disagree. I may not at a given time be in possession of the truth, but there is such a thing as the truth. All opinions and behaviors are not equally valid. It matters what a person believes for there are consequences. Just as Oskar Schindler had to do what he believed was right, I too owe it to Our Father to stand up for my convictions, even when doing so puts me at odds with certain others. And I am without a doubt called to do so when some of God's children are treating others of God's children as though they are Urins.

Followers of Jesus should always be dubious allies of any political party or special interest group, any subdivision of Our. Ours is not to follow the party line blindly, as happened in Germany under Hitler. Jesus is Lord of the conscience, the One to whom I am answerable. I am not ultimately answerable to the Democrats or the Republicans, to the left or right, to biological family or race or flag. No group is right all the time.

The Lord's Prayer is a life-changing, world-changing prayer. In essence, H.G. Wells recognized this. H.G. Wells, who wrote *War of the Worlds*, was an historian and author who did not think of himself as a Christian. Still, he considered Jesus, the man, to be the most important person to ever have lived.

"That place is his by virtue of the… profound ideas which he released – the profound importance of the individual under the Fatherhood of God and the conception of the kingdom of heaven.

"It is one of the most revolutionary changes of outlook that has ever stirred and changed human thought. No age has even yet understood fully the tremendous challenge it carries…But the world began to be a different world from the day that doctrine was preached and every step toward wider understanding and tolerance and good will is a step in the direction of that universal brotherhood Christ proclaimed.

"The historian's test of an individual's greatness is, 'What did he leave to grow? Did he start men to thinking along fresh lines with a vigor that persisted after him?' By this test Jesus stands first." (4)

Appendix I

The Temptation of Jesus

As stated earlier, the Temptation of Jesus in Matthew 4: 1-11 illustrates portions of The Lord's Prayer.

Then Jesus was led up by the Spirit into the wilderness to be tempted by the devil. He fasted forty days and forty nights, and afterwards he was famished. The tempter came and said to him, "If you are the son of God, command these stones to become loaves of bread."

Jesus answered the tempter, *"It is written, 'One does not live by bread alone, but by every word that comes from the mouth of God.'"* And Jesus teaches us to pray, "Give us this day our daily bread," spiritual sustenance. See Chapter 10.

Then the devil took him to the holy city and placed him on the pinnacle of the temple, saying to him, "If you are the Son of God, throw yourself down; for it is written, 'He will command his angels concerning you,' and 'On their hands they will bear you up, so that you will not dash your foot against a stone.'"

Jesus answered the devil, *"Again it is written, 'Do not put the Lord your God to the test.'"* And Jesus teaches us to pray, "Lead us not into temptation," the act of tempting God to go along with our agenda. See Chapter 12.

Again, the devil took him to a very high mountain and showed him all the kingdoms of the world and their splendor; and he said to him, *"All these I will give you, if you will fall down and worship me."*

Jesus said to the devil, *"Away with you, Satan! For it is written, 'Worship the Lord your God, and serve only him.'"* And Jesus tells us to pray, "Thy will be done." We cannot serve God using the ways of the world. See Chapter 7.

Appendix II

Where Do The Words Come From?

Of all the words that Jesus could have weaved into a prayer to teach his followers, where in their common experience do these words come from?

In large measure, they come from the Exodus story, the central event of the Hebrew Bible. To free the Hebrews from slavery in Egypt, Moses first asks that God reveal His name (*Hallow your name*) so he can tell his people who sent him. Moses then leads the Hebrews from life under Pharoah's rule toward life under God's rule in the Promised Land (*Your kingdom come*). Along the way, in the wilderness, God teaches the people his ways (*Your will be done*).

Jesus reveals or *hallows* God's name in TLP as Our Father, in heaven. Jesus is leading us from life under the present regime to life fully under God's rule, *Your kingdom come.* And Jesus teaches us to pray along the way, *Your will be done.* The Exodus story was ingrained in Jesus and his people, and it serves as a backdrop for TLP. There is even a correspondence between the chronology of the Book of Exodus and the ordering of events in the Gospel of Matthew leading up to The Lord's Prayer:

Exodus Chronology	Matthew's Order
The birth of Moses	The birth of Jesus
Baby Moses eludes death at the hand of Pharoah	Baby Jesus eludes death at the hand of Herod

Crossing the Red Sea	Baptism of Jesus
The Temptation of God by the people	The Temptation of Jesus by Satan
Giving the law at Mt. Sinai	Sermon on the Mount, including The Lord's Prayer

Appendix III

Table Format

Tables were used in ancient times, the left-hand column matching up with the right-hand column. I am of the opinion that this is the format of The Lord's Prayer, and for this reason I matched the petitions as I did in chapters 9-11.

Our Father, in heaven,

(1) Hallow your name	*(4) Give us this day our daily bread*
(2) Your kingdom come	*(5) And forgive us our debts as we forgive our debtors*
(3) Your will be done	*(6) Lead us not into Temptation*
On earth as it is in Heaven (1-3)	*But deliver us from evil (4-6)*

....

In the original Greek of TLP, the verb mood of all six petitions is imperative, i.e., I'm not begging a stingy God to put things right. No blood out of a turnip here. Nor am I cajoling or coaxing a God who has something better to do than work for the wellbeing of humankind and creation. In no way am I asking Our Father to act contrary to His nature. In the first three petitions, I'm stating my support, encouraging and exhorting God to carry through with what God has been doing, is doing, and will be doing until life as we know it is transformed into the new world coming. "Go for it, Our Father! I'm with you and I'm for you!"

The qualifier, *On earth as it is in heaven,* applies to the first three petitions, not to the third only.

In the second three petitions, 4-6, I join with Jesus' church, the *Us* in the prayer, in confidently asking for what I need to be put right with God as God moves the world toward the kingdom of heaven. Again, I am asking for nothing that God isn't on record as providing. I ask because God will help me in these ways.

The qualifier, *But deliver us from evil,* applies to the second three petitions, not to just petition six.

Furthermore, the second set of petitions dovetails with the first set in table-like fashion, 4-1, 5-2, and 6-3.

To pray *Hallow your name* (1) obligates me to also pray *Give us this day our daily bread (no more)* (4).

Make your kingdom come (2) necessitates *Forgive us our debts as we forgive our debtors* (5).

Demand your will be done (3) requires *Lead us not to the point where we tempt You with our agenda* (6).

Another way of looking at the structure of TLP is like this (Read columns from top to bottom:

Our Father, in heaven

I support Your	Thus, I need
Doing these	Your help in
Three things	these three ways
So life on earth	To be put right
will come fully	with you and
under your rule	and be delivered
	from all that
	opposes You.

References

1. *Simone Weil,* Francine Du Plessix Gray, Penguin Group, 2001.
2. Tony Campolo, from the video course, *What's So Amazing About Grace?*, Philip Yancey, Zondervan, 2000.
3. *Schindler's List,* Universal Pictures, 1993.
4. H.G. Wells, "The Three Greatest Men in History," from *The Seventh Trumpet,* Mark Link, Argus Communications, 1978.